Veterans' Voices

*Personal Reflections on the
Freedom Wars and Beyond*

Compiled and Edited

by

Kevin Lewis

Vision Spots Publishing

A Service Unit of

LMK Partners LLC

Copyright Notice

Contents

Preface

Operation Iraqi Freedom and Operation Enduring Freedom...the Freedom Wars. America has been on this war footing since 2001. With this has come a new generation of veteran warriors, many of whom are now transitioning back into civilian life.

I have had privilege of mentoring five of these Warrior Veterans. The common thread through this experience was the realization that a major disconnect exists between this community and the general public. It was very difficult to watch how these veterans were struggling to make it through this transition. Misinformation and stereotypical thinking often impeded a good understanding of what these veterans could bring to table.

I decided to reach out to the broader community and invite veterans to share their backgrounds and experiences. This book captures these interviews and presents them as simple, straightforward stories. Of course they are a microscopic representation of the vast number of stories across America. My hope is that this book will shine an informative light on what this community has borne for this country and what value they can bring to their communities.

Kevin Lewis
Author, Business Owner, &
Vietnam-era Veteran

Foreword

The warrior culture is very distinct. It embodies a set of character traits and a lifestyle unparalleled in the civilian world. Integrity, sense of duty, loyalty, respect, discipline, courage, and selflessness are not just cliché "words we live by", but actual values instilled within this culture. And although none of these values are unique to the military, they take on new meaning for our servicemen and women who live a life of multiple deployments and all the challenges that come with being in combat and away from their families for extended periods of time.

With the United Stated military winding down the longest war in its history we see more and more men and women from this warrior class reintegrating back into civilian society. With this special class of people comes a unique set of challenges when returning home.

We live in a society that has been virtually untouched by the war and few have direct contact with the veterans community. In fact, less than one half of one percent of the American population serves in the military. This fraction of our society has taken on the entire burden of serving in our two recent conflicts. This creates a disconnect between the rest of society and the warrior class that serves them.

Because of this, stigmas and assumptions abound. *Veterans' Voices* helps break down some of these negative stereotypes created by the media and movies. This work you are about to read will allow you to hear the voices of the veterans and what their challenges are. And even though they return from war with special challenges that we must address they also possess special talents that we should embrace.

This book helps put a face to our warriors and gives them a voice for us to learn from. Most importantly, it gives you a glimpse of who they are and why they are a great benefit to the business sector. My hope is that the business community will benefit from this work and be better equipped to help veterans with the transition back into the work force. *Veterans' Voices* helps us see the value of bringing veterans to the workforce.

Christopher Loverro
Iraq War Veteran, US Army
Actor, Writer, Filmmaker

Raised in Oakland, California and a Graduate of UC Berkeley's Peace and Conflict Studies department, Christopher Loverro is a former police officer and Iraq War veteran turned actor and independent filmmaker.

While working as a Berkeley Police Officer, Christopher joined the Army Reserves in 2001 and volunteered for a deployment to Iraq in 2003-2004. He served on a Civil Affairs team in support of the Army's first Stryker Brigade Combat Team (3-2) in Mosul, Iraq. Among various other missions he helped conducted humanitarian relief operations for over 2,000 refugees.

Ironically, after surviving his year in Iraq, he returned to his job as a police officer and was injured in the line-of-duty while fighting a kidnapper. This eventually cut his law enforcement career short.

He then attended film school to learn how to tell stories about veterans and the sacrifice they and their families make. Using the Post 9/11 GI Bill, he studied acting and discovered it can be a great form of catharsis.

Christopher is trying to use acting and filmmaking to promote awareness about veteran's issues and to promote these arts to veterans as an alternative form of therapy for dealing with PTSD.

His short film *Journey Home,* for which he served as writer, director, and actor, was recognized by the GI Film Festival in 2011.

Introduction

America has been at war for over a decade. Many of our nation's military have been deployed multiple times in service to our country. This has not come without difficulties for them personally, and now professionally, as many of them prepare to transition from military to civilian life. As a nation, we are now facing the largest drawdown of our military since the Cold War. This drawdown and transition process brings many challenges and opportunities.

Some of these challenges include a society who, for the most part, only knows about the military through the lens of our media, entertainment, or culture. Sadly most Americans today have little direct contact with veterans. Many erroneous assumptions are made about the veteran community which, unwittingly, add more unnecessary obstacles to a process that is already arduous for many.

Veterans today have experienced the appreciation that many Americans willingly and gladly express. But unfortunately when these same veterans begin the process of seeking new careers, they encounter situations within the business community that give them pause and cause them to question how real the expressions of appreciation and desire to help truly are.

The purpose of this book is to, first and foremost, capture in their own words the experiences that some of today's veterans have had as they have navigated through their transitions. Secondly, it will provide the business community with a better understanding and unfiltered view of the veteran community. Finally, for the veteran community itself, hopefully this book will offer some candid advice and guidance as each veteran makes his/her way into a new season of life.

Chapter 1: Their Experience Will Bring Great Value

*Meet **John Boerstler**, Texan, combat Marine Veteran, now serving with the Wounded Warrior Project*

John, would you just take a few moments here and talk about your hometown background and those things that led you into the military?

I grew up in southwest Houston. I always wanted to do something more than everyone else did, to serve my country. I wasn't interested in going straight to college like a lot of my friends did.

I needed something greater than myself. I had served in Boy Scouts, church groups and other service related organizations in high school. That motivated me to search for something higher. So that's why I joined the Marine Corps.

When you first entered the military, what surprises, if any, did you encounter?

There were many challenges when you enter the military, especially when you're so young. I guess I was more surprised by the way it operated. I really enjoy the culture. I love and I enjoy the difficulty. I enjoy the discipline. My career field was infantry.

There is so much downtime and there is so much other unrelated stuff that happened to me. Some of it I will call 'politics'. It's what inevitably led me to decide to not pursue a career.

Tell me about where you were deployed and about your mission.

We were deployed in support of Operation Iraqi Freedom to conduct counterinsurgency operations. This was one deployment. We were also sent on another peace-keeping mission in the Republic of Kenya.

Looking back at your time in the service what would you say was your darkest moment or your deepest challenge that you experienced while on active duty?

I would say it was when two marine helicopters during a sandstorm, killing 26 fellow marines. We had to go police the crash site. That's when I really grew up.

How did your fellow Marines handle this and how did it affect you?

As I see it overall, it was the lack of decompression time that has affected us adversely, as I look back. Earlier other generations had significant decompression times in-between their combat deployments.

For our generation, we can be in Afghanistan or Iraq one day and thirty six hours later, we can be back at home with spouse and kids. Many back home don't know what we have been through. So conflict and stress at home can be a big problem because we have not had time to decompress and adjust. For some, that is when emotional or mental issues can become a problem. The only physical injuries I suffered was trauma to my right eye from a radio antennae going into it which healed up actually quite nicely during my deployment. I officially got out of the service in October 2006.

Talk about your transition to civilian life.

I went back to college and finished my degree. I made a lot of new friends and had actually a pretty healthy transition. I had really no interaction with veterans. All my friends were civilians and they were great people.

When I got out of college, I started

working for a congressman. Of course naturally they assigned me to handle all of the military and veterans affairs issues. I did some field work, going out and representing the office, finding out what the community needs, and bringing it back to the congressman. After that, I served two and half years working for the city of Houston in the mayor's office. I continued in the field of military and veterans affairs. I started a returning veteran initiative. Our mission was to connect all the various non-profits and identify resources to help our veterans.

From there I was recruited to serve with the Wounded Warrior Project in March 2011 to start a new program, a public awareness campaign. This led to a position that opened up in Houston to manage the Gulf coast program, which is what I do now.

I also helped to start the Lone Star Veteran's Association which is a network of over five thousand Iraq and Afghanistan veterans and families here in the Houston area. It's a non-profit organization for which I now serve on the board of directors.

Based on what you're observing, experiencing and witnessing with today's warrior veterans, what would you like people in general to know that they may not be aware of?

We know that approximately forty-eight thousand of us have been wounded and some were injured seriously. But we also now know according to the Rand Corporation's recent survey that four hundred thousand veterans now suffer from combat and stress related issues, which include post-traumatic stress disorder, depression, and isolation. There are also wounds of our war such as traumatic brain injury that have resulted in severe headaches and memory loss.

But reflecting on the comment that I made about decompression time, I think it's important for the public to understand that veterans are serving multiple deployments. They are coming home without the amount of decompression that they really and truly need to recover and heal mentally, emotionally and physically. Then, when they get home, they start training to go back or they get out of the service and don't have much of a purpose anymore. That's when veterans struggle.

For your transition, as you look back, did you have any challenges making your own personal transition from military civilian life?

Absolutely! I dealt with not knowing what I was going to do and not having that purpose. I had substance abuse issues and a couple of run-ins with the law. I learned a lot from that experience. But most importantly I think I learned a lot about the plight of other veterans who didn't have a support system or a community of resources that I did. This is what compelled me into doing what I do now. Knowing how to navigate the system successfully, I need to pass that on and I need to help them make that successful transition from military to civilian life. To be honest with you, that's the best therapy, helping a veteran determine his or her life mission.

If you were talking to some business owners and you wanted them to know something about today's soldiers, what would you want them to know, to remember about soldiers as theses business people make their own judgment about considering veterans as potential employees?

They need to know that these young veterans have been in charge of government equipment, dozens of personnel, and were responsible for people's lives everyday day. A non-veteran, college graduate has never had such an experience. A veteran may be applying for just a regular blue collar job in a civilian workforce, something that he or she may be over qualified for. Nonetheless, their experience will bring great value to any organization. They will show up early and they will stay late. They will work three times harder and they will show you respect while doing it.

Let me put you in a room of

veterans leaving the service. They are getting ready to make this transition and move to this new season in their life. What would you want them to know? What would you tell them to think about as they make their transition?

Whatever resources you received from the military during your transition are helpful. But what you really need to know is what resources exist in your community. Veterans need to examine and become aware of those organizations within their own home communities that can provide resources and support for the transition to the new life in front of them.

There is so much that you can learn from making that successful transition from military to civilian life. The DOD is not necessarily going to give you that. Their mission is to train soldiers and protect the United States. Their mission is not to make sure that those soldiers make a successful transition.

So if I was sitting in a room with a bunch of other veterans who just got out, I would say to take the information that is available through these other non-profit resources and use it, take advantage of it.

What personal goals do you have over the next five years?

My major personal goals are to take care of my family, to make sure that my wife and I have enough income to buy a bigger house where we can have kids. I want to have a job that's fulfilling. I want to be passionate about my work. I want to care about it and I want to see results.

I never thought I would be working in this industry. I have turned down a couple of jobs outside the industry. This means a lot to me.

I can see that it does. I applaud your passion and desire to serve our veterans. Let me thank you again for your service and for being a part of this project.

Chapter 2: Keep Advocating

*Meet **Curtis Fluitt**, Texan, Air Force Veteran, now serving with the Salvation Army*

Curtis, again thanks for being a part of this. You were actually a big part of pulling a lot of people together for this project. Let me just say thank you. Listen, why don't we start off by just talking about your background. Talk about your hometown experience.

Okay I grew up in a Katy, Texas. I was born in Houston and grew up in Katy. I lived there my entire life. At seventeen I graduated high school early and decided to enlist in the Air-Force. I had to wait until my eighteenth birthday. As soon as I turned eighteen, I was gone within the next two weeks to boot camp. That's how I got started. I grew up in a small town and had a lot of family and support around me.

My dad was in the Navy. My grandfather was in Korea. My other grandfather was in World War II. So I heard a lot of military history growing up as well. So I wanted to live on that legacy and leave that to my family.

Sounds like you had a lot of encouragement and a lot of history in your family. Is that what was the motivation for you to enter the service?

I never really wanted to go to college right away. So I thought the military would be a good building block for my foundation. I did have my family support behind me. So there was definitely no flack as far as joining the military.

Were there any surprises after

entering? What were your thoughts after you entered the military?

I knew I had to learn on my own, to adapt to a new culture because the language was different. So that was my surprise. There was no feeling of home. It was pretty much a culture shock from the minute I left Houston. I got to San Antonio and went into an open mechanical position. I didn't know what job I was going to have. My whole career was play–by-ear type of situation. The whole situation was kind of a surprise after I left the Houston area.

As you look back at that now, do you feel as if there might have been some way you might have prepared better?

I think I would have paid attention more to my surroundings. A lot of it came down to listening and being prepared. If I had paid attention, I would have been more aware of my surroundings. I would have had a lot easier time in my initial adjustment to the military. So I would have definitely paid more attention and thought more about what it was I was doing as I entered the military. Looking back, I kind of closed my eyes and jumped in

Share your military background, your profile of service.

I was originally listed as active duty Air Force. I was active duty for three years and two months. I injured my back when I was in Iraq and returned to a desk-type position.

I wanted to retrain and had the opportunity to transfer into the Air Force reserves. So I wound up changing jobs but staying at the same location. I was in California at the time. That is where I wanted to be. So I went ahead and transferred into the Air Force reserves.

I was in the Air Force reserves in California and in Colorado until 2009 and then I separated. After my contract was up, I moved back to Houston. My inactive reserve time which was a total of nine years ended in April 2012.

So you've been in all dimensions of

service.

Yes sir I've seen all three different sides. You know it's interesting to see all different aspects of how the active component and the reserve component work and how they work together.

Now you were deployed to Iraq four months, correct?

Yes sir... I was in Iraq from June 2005 until October two 2005

Did you suffer an injury?

I did. It was kind of self-inflicted at the time but it was also due to indirect fire. I was a mechanic. One evening and I was going to get my toolbox over the line prior to taking shelter and, as I did that, I injured my back as I tried to pick it up and run at the same time. So after that happened I was came back to the States and basically was told in the VA that it was to be a chronic injury that I would have the rest of my life. I would have to manage it. I was told that it would never get better. But there was no real fix for the injury.

How are you doing now as far as that injury is concerned?

You know, it's been a lot better. I've been doing a lot of pain management. I've done a lot of Yoga. I've done a lot of taking it easy. I don't do nearly what I used to do as far as physical exercise. Otherwise I still remain active. You know I still try to be a part of the community and to be an outreach person. I don't fix planes anymore I don't work under cars anymore. I really try and watch my movements and my posture to stay healthy.

As you look back, what was a deep challenge or maybe even a dark moment that you may have experienced while you were in the service?

That is really a two-fold question. One part was experiencing the separation from family. I mean I think everybody goes through that thing. You look at your orders and ticket and realize that you are on a one-way trip with really no idea when you're back coming home. So that was one the kind of kind a hit me. The other part was actually getting orders to Iraq and knowing that you will really be in harm's way. It hits you that you may not be going back home. It was realizing that we are at the tip of the sphere.

Let's talk about your transition back. Talk about how that was for you as you transitioned from to civilian life.

Well I got married in the military. So I had support as I initially transitioned. I was married to another Air Force member. She had me supported to a point to where I felt comfortable enough transitioning out. But at that time she was deploying as well. So even though I had the support at home, she wasn't home to really support me. It was still looking difficult without having someone to return to. I kind of felt alone and isolated to where there was no hope around me. I floundered, not knowing where to turn.

My transition was difficult but I found a way to kind of push through and navigate the system to where I got my college degree. I was able to make a name for myself in the community and find organizations that can help me adapt and overcome the transition process which is where I'm at now.

Tell me about the work you're currently doing.

I took a job two weeks ago with the Salvation Army to support veterans' families. We are doing community outreach to fund sixty percent of veterans who are literally homeless. We're looking to get them off the street or to keep them in their current housing. So it's basically an effort to let the veterans know that we care.

Let me ask you about that homeless situation. That is just so disturbing to me. I've been aware of it but nonetheless. It is just very disturbing. Tell me what is happening there. What are you seeing in terms of what's happening with veterans who are falling into that homelessness situation.

We conducted a national stand-down day for veterans whereby any veteran who has a home-related or other service issue can meet at one location in Houston and get assistance. So we had two hundred agencies in place to assist those with housing issues, medical issues, immunization, disability claims. You name the issue and we had the agency there to support them. What I'm finding is that the Vietnam generation and the Desert Storm generation of veterans are also finding themselves unable to keep their current housing. Every veteran that showed up got a pair of combat boots, a duffle bag, a back pack, and any kind of hygiene products they wanted to keep themselves clean on the street, as well as access to a closing closet.

They were able get interviews, to get off the street, or just to be together. In Houston, we have over thirty thousand veterans in the city alone. The homeless situation is very chronic. We are trying to raise the awareness of this situation, to get them help that they need and to re-establish them in the community.

That is wonderful work. It hurts me to hear that's happening. I know it exists. That's why I wanted to ask you about it. No veteran just one day turns homeless overnight. I'm sure there's a series of things that happen. What do you feel the root cause or causes are?

What I find the most is mismanagement of funds. For the older veterans such as the Vietnam era vets, it has been PTSD. There was no assistance for them when they returned and this has taken its toll. I've also realized that substance abuse plays a part. It's not really the driving factor that drives them to the streets. But once they get into a desperate or isolated state of mind, they use drugs and alcohol to cope with their situation. This causes a downward spiral into bad decision-making which can bring on homelessness. Loss of family or separation between wife and husband that causes instability is also an issue. They may be living on two incomes. They lose one and that throws them into a tail spin.

What are you looking at for the future? What are aspirations do you have?

My ultimate goal is to maintain a social service type of career field. The more that I work with the veteran community, the more that I see myself looking community partnerships. So I may not be behind the desk doing case work forever. But I do see myself being involved with the same type of population and try to get them the services they need. I think that I can definitely be an advocate. Being a veteran myself and going through the VA system and understanding where they coming from, being able to exercise and get myself in their shoes. I have an ability that not everyone has. There is one percent of a city served and even less than that are in this type of situation. So if I can be a voice to them and guide them to the services they need, that's where I see my passion going. So that's what I'm planning on doing.

I've had a number of conversations with business people. They admire what the military has done. What would you want them to understand about military people? What would you say to local businesses that you would want them to understand about that community of people?

I have done a couple of different presentations on the military. I have outlined reasons why the veteran community is an attractive community. Veterans are not broken. They are dedicated individuals who are there to serve. So by hiring a veteran, you are getting someone who is adaptable, who learns quickly, and is committed to getting the job done. They are a community who knows how to handle stress and still perform under great stress. They are tried and true and can bring a great value to your business.

Let me ask you about the next five or more years. If you're looking out five to ten years from now, what are some long term goals that you want to achieve?

I'd like to have my graduate degree within the next two to three. From there I'd like to maintain the social service network and be a community partner whether it be my own non-profit or working for another one to keep helping and bettering the community.

I've done a lot of work with different non-profits around the country and around the local area as well. The more I see the work that they do, the more I want to continue and help build those networks. So that's what I see myself doing for the next five to ten years.

Let me ask you this last question. If you had one shot at communicating with the veteran and business communities and had to sum up a message that you wanted them to not forget, what would it be?

For the veteran community, if they don't remember anything else, it would be to keep advocating for themselves. You have to be your own boss and you have to stand for what you believe in. You've already done it once by saving your country. Now it's your turn again. You've earned those rights and those benefits. So keep advocating and eventually you'll be able to obtain what it is you're looking for. For the business community, don't ignore the veteran community. Don't believe everything you hear in the media. Meet with and talk with them. They can be an asset to your enterprise. Don't be fearful or worried about a condition they may or not have. Give them a chance.

Curtis, this has been wonderful. Thank you for contributing as you have and for assisting in pulling other veterans together. And...thank you for stepping into harm's way for our country.

Chapter 3: Be Pragmatic

*Meet **Dave Nieman**, Californian, Desert Storm Navy Veteran, now serving as an educator*

Dave, let's start by talking about your background, your hometown experience and the reasons that drew you into the military.

I was a born California, then moved to South Jersey. During my middle school years, we moved to Pennsylvania. I think my mom agonized over the fact that this was traumatic for a little boy making all of these moves. I actually thought it was great. I was always excited. I think that it really provided a psychological backdrop, so to speak, for moving in and transitioning into new environments.

I did quite well in high school. Better socially than academically. However as graduation approached, I realized I was woefully ill-prepared for life after high school. Some of that had to do with my Dad. He was a workaholic but that's not a character flaw. He was a great provider. We did a lot of great things together. But there was never a real push in the house talking about life after graduation. One day, I was driving home and I remember pulling into a parking lot next to a recruiting station. I just sat there and I thought "I'm going to give the U.S. military a fair shake." I spoke with several recruiters and ended up enlisting in the Navy. I was in the Navy for four years from nineteen ninety to ninety four.

Were there any surprises? Was there anything that, when you look back, you realized you were not really prepared for?

Looking back, I would say that what challenged me were the mental demands. Keeping on track with the intensive temp of boot camp and the instructions that I had to stay on track with.

What would you say has been your darkest moment or the deepest challenge that you had either while you were in the military or maybe even since then?

I really think that for me some of the most challenging moments really came at a spiritual level. I began to wrestle with God. I began to meet some people. There were two in particular that stood out. They had become very devout Christians. They were very sincere in their faith. When we would talk and hang out, they would say or do things differently. I noticed right away. I recall saying "there is something different about you" or "you're a Christian aren't you?"

I was born and raised in a church. I was kind of a nominal, lukewarm believer. But suddenly I guess I realized that there were people that were actually taking ownership of their faith. The parallel would be back to my Navy school experience. I needed to take ownership for my success. When I awakened to that, I realized that I could do it. While my grades were superior, they improved remarkably.

I should mention that one of the high watermarks was that my ship would actually be in the Persian Gulf War, Desert Storm. Desert shield had just unfolded as I was graduating high school and moving into boot camp.

It was at that time that I heard a deep rustle about really giving my life to Christ. I did make that decision.

So I've been incredibly blessed. I've had career ups and other trials that I faced. It kind of reminded me of the book of James. "We're to consider all of our trials as gold because they refine and perfect our faith".

Let me just jump in here Dave and say that I'm a believer. It is very encouraging to hear you share your faith. It's wonderful and encouraging to me. Let me go back to your transition out of the military. Share what your transition was like. What hurdles did you have?

I had made the decision to get out of the Navy and go to school. I needed to have a plan. I thought back to my high school days when I did not have a plan. So I took steps this time to get prepared for my exit from the service. I went to the library and started researching schools. I wanted to get my college degree and thought I could do so in a school in San Diego. I sent away for brochures. After leaving the navy in San Diego, I remember just taking off a half day and driving up on a college campus and walking in the front door just like I did for the recruiters. I got some information and started walking around the campus. The lesson learned here is to do your research. Be prepared to find out what you need to do to fill in the gaps within your skills.

Are you involved in working with service members in any way, whether it be voluntary or otherwise?

In an informal sense I certainly do. I do so through my church. I encourage service members to be pragmatic with their choices. I encourage them to not look at any of their problems through only one dimension.

If you were talking to the business community about veterans, what would you tell them about the veteran community?

I'd say there are intrinsic qualities in a veteran that are valuable assets to your organization. Overlook the fact that they may not often be degreed or have a certification. Look for actual character. By character I mean if someone has had successful years in the military, such as the four years I had, they can bring value to your organization. There has to be a level of integrity and honesty.

So if what you need is a person that you can nurture him, the veteran would say "Absolutely! I might not have the degree and the credential and the license or these types of things, but I am trainable."

Veterans also need to list their awards when applying for positions. This will highlight their value and experience.

Share the work you're doing now and where you see yourself in the next five years.

I completed college and worked for the Smithsonian. Later I worked as a substitute teacher. I figured out how to get to the school. I got there on time. I dressed appropriately. I took charge of the class. The lesson plans were well prepared. I wrote my name on the board and I looked at the students straight in the eyes. I took charge of the class and the students resonated with it. I loved it. I taught for ten years.

I later moved into instructional design work. Essentially what that means is developing curriculum for organizations. So these are certain government contracts and companies that look for these types of services. They hire folks like me to help write and create curriculum. Of course as an educator with a masters in education, I've got a lot of skills and experience in how to craft curriculum. That is what I am currently doing.

Are there things that you would like to accomplish outside of your career?

I have a four year old. He is top priority. I want and need to be the father that he needs. So I guess on a personal level, I need to be sure that I'm not so burdened with commitments elsewhere that my son is somewhere down the list. He's really a top priority and that takes discipline to say no to things. So I guess on a personal family level, I need to be the husband and father what God wants me to be. As I am building my resume in this instructional design area, perhaps one day I will open my own business as an independent consultant. Those are the two things that I see on the horizon.

Let me also say that I believe the nation is waking up to toll that war is having on its service members. The biggest toll is on those coming home, having just been on the frontlines, now enduring the challenges of getting their lives back in order.

You're right. The nation is waking up. I am concerned about veterans who may slip through the cracks like they did during Vietnam. I am glad you are out there doing your part. Thank you for your service to them and to the nation.

Chapter 4: You Will Get There

*Meet **Jim Roos**, Texan, Army Veteran, now serving with the Wounded Warrior Project*

Jim, talk about your background, talk about your hometown experience and what led you into stepping into the military.

I grew up in San Antonio. I always wanted to be a soldier when I grew up, so I joined 1985 the first time. I was a tanker and I went to Germany. I served along the East German border. I then went to Fort Stewart, did a couple of NTC rotations. I was a specialist when I got out. I went to college and started working at a golf course as a golf course mechanic on the road to becoming an agronomist and a golf course manager, which is something I didn't really aspire to do. I just kind of fell into that. I was really, really bored, so I decided I'd join again. I said "This time I want to do it right." So I joined the infantry, went to airborne school, went to ranger school. Later I served in a military intelligence unit. That was a core asset that spoke to the commander about what was going on in the battlefield. I'm married and I have three boys 20, 18 and 12 and I live here now in Houston.

Well, that's interesting that you served twice. I've known people who've done that. Were there any surprises either the first or the second time going into the military? You know, things that if you look back at, maybe you reflect on it now and you might have prepared better.

I was probably not in as good a shape when I re-entered the service because I was living a civilian life. But I worked hard and I got through all that. That was probably the biggest surprise. Later, I was injured in a plane crash at the airport in North Carolina in March 23rd 1994. That's why I got out at an odd time. I was in the airport space crash. I was in the hospital for 66 days.

OK. And so after that, what was your status?

I was wounded. I was in transition to leave the service. The basic steps were to get your treatment done, go see the VA, and then leave the service if that was your status. It was a lot different than it is now.

I'm assuming you had extensive treatments, recovery, and rehabilitation. Would you mind sharing to what degree you were injured?

I had third degree burns over 43% of my body. My major injuries were my hands and my face and my head in the right side of my body. The plane landed and bounced through our formation on the right hand side of my body, so I had to roll myself around on the ground to put myself out. I did all that and they put us on the medevac to Womack Army

Hospital at Fort Bragg. That's about all I remember. I woke up in San Antonio.

Let me ask you a kind of a piercing question here. What has been your darkest moment or any deep challenge you've experienced?

I would have to say that it was experiencing the severe change in my physical condition and learning to live with it. Prior to the crash, I was in tremendous shape...like an Olympic athlete. That's the vanity of it all. I was super strong, bulletproof. We would do stupid stuff like treading water in a swimming pool for hours to see who could go the longest. We would walk 50 miles in a couple of days. Looking back on it, it's just amazing. Now my physical condition includes crippled hands and other limitations. I still do a lot. I still ride my motorcycle.

I'm a professional now, assisting guys that are in transition. I work on my VA credits. I'm a representative, so I'm kind of an office guy now. But even that office guy is a little bit out of the norm for me, but I enjoy it because I believe that we have to care for these guys getting out. I don't really have a whole lot of mental anguish over the whole thing. For me, I was doing a parachute jump that day and had a bad day at the office. I don't have a lot of blame or hurt, just mainly the physical transitioning from the physical injuries for me was my main thing. That and going through the burn treatment. That was really tough.

I guess I moved along quickly from one thing to the next. I had to change direction quickly, so I was already checking out colleges and stuff like that while I was going through a lot of my active treatment. I went to a private Catholic college. I really, really appreciated that kind of education. And that led me into the career path that I have now, which I enjoy. It's a top job. I'm an accredited VA representative, to help guys who transition all the way through.

As you work with today's transitioning soldiers, what would you want to tell the business world about

these soldiers and what they bring to the table?

Well, what the business community can do is they need to hire these guys. Use their military skills to the company's advantage. And these guys are really good. Some guys get on that Government cheese and they don't want to get off. And I think that is a challenge... Businesses should invite veterans for a field day at their office or something like that, to show them that they have a lot of work. Veterans really need to work. As veterans leave the service, it's my job to make sure they get the maximum amount of disability possible. I have several guys that are 100%...they can't be working. That's understandable. Other guys get up to a certain percentage and say "I'm good, I've got social security. I've got VA compensation and I'm going to just stay home and go fishing." It's terrible and it's a big problem right now that I see.

I have been hearing that there was this kind of a tipping point situation where some soldiers, given their young age and not being

married, could see their way of living their lives without having to go back and engage in the workforce. There was enough money coming in and depending upon where they lived in the country, they could live on their income. And what I began to see was that some of these soldiers who started out that way began to slowly spiral downwards. They're young and they still have their whole lives in front of them and they want to accomplish things and they're not doing that. And that's what I was beginning to see. Is that kind of what your experience has been?

Yes. We are working to get these veterans exposed to other environments where they can see challenges and opportunities to grow. It is vital for them to understand what is out there in order to prevent them from spiralling downward with no purpose. Iraq was a game changer for these guys. Afghanistan, as well. The constant angst that these guys were in in Iraq was tremendous. Those guys went to war and they were doing horrible stuff all the time. It really changed them and they get very isolated. We work to challenge that and to have them come out, to get out and do stuff with us, do activities, events. We are making a difference, but there's a lot of work to be done. These soldiers have to deal with being medicated, drinking, drugging. We have to pull them out of that.

How long have you been working in this capacity with the Wounded Warriors?

I've started with the WWP approximately in November 2010, but prior to that, as soon as I got out, I was in college, I was a work study for the VA in the late '90s. Then I was a supervisor of the Disabled American Veterans office in San Antonio and they asked me if I wanted to do that kind of work. So I said "Sure". Then I started that in 1998 to 2010, when I started with Wounded Warrior Project.

And this is the same Wounded Warrior Project we see advertised on television, correct?

Yes, sir. I'm in the professional arm of WWP.

Well, Jim, let me ask you this: you're in this new, what I would say, great, exciting service-minded season of life right now. When you look out over the next few years, what do you want to accomplish or what do you want to see accomplished? What kinds of things do you think you want to get done or see get done here over the next few years?

I think the next few years we need to revisit some of the guys from early '03, '04 and '05. There's a ton of guys out there, both men and women, who got out and are a little bit lost right now. I want to continue to work in this area and help them through our events and our outside activities to bring them back into the VA. The WWP gets these guys to the front door of the VA. There's a ton of really great people that work in the VA and they want to help and they want to do good, but the warrior, the veteran has to get there. I think the WWP will still be very instrumental in accomplishing that, bridging that gap between the Government and the warrior and the veteran.

Also we need to get these guys working. We need to get them continuing obviously on the transition side. Our WWP wants to have this be the greatest generation of warriors ever. Really challenging the WW2 generation, to take this country forward into the global economy. Also, we haven't seen as bad as it's going to get yet. We're going to have so many guys transitioning into the VA, into the workforce, into the education system. I have a presence at several universities in the greater Houston area, where I'm just there to benefit guys working with the VA counsellors. So really it's more into making sure these guys don't drink and drug. They need to stay out of that kind of stuff.

Let me paint two pictures to kind of close out with, Jim, and I want you to respond to each of these. First, you're talking to a group of business people. I've heard business people say "You know what, I want to help

veterans. I'm a small business. I want to do something. I don't have a lot of money, but I want to engage with this community." That's what I'm hearing from a lot of business people. So you are talking to a room full of small business owners or business people and you want them to remember some key things about how they can connect to this community. What would you want them to remember?

I would have them reach out to their local WWP office and have them volunteer with the soldiers and the marines in some kind of event. Helping with the fishing tournament, helping with the dinners, the families. Have some quiet conversations as they build these relationships with our staff and seeing what the warriors need in their areas. And just start building a relationship with us. I think the WWP is the best blend between the professional side and the fun-side.

You make an excellent point. I was in a meeting the other day with a

small group of local business people and this was exactly what was coming out, that they just want to make some personal connections and just have some unfiltered access to people so that they can hear and see what the needs are.

Let me go to the other picture. The last picture I wanted to paint here was this: you're talking to warriors, soldiers, veterans and you're talking to them candidly. They want you to speak straight, tell them straight, give it to them straight so they know what to do. Most of them are mission-focused. They just say "Tell me what to do." What key things would you say to them? What would you want them to remember?

To the soldiers I would have them remember that it's not easy. I would tell them that they are home now. Yes...it was bad down range. But now you are home. I would remind them that if they see someone with the trappings of success, to remember that they worked hard to achieve that. You worked hard in the service. Work hard now. Use your discipline and work ethic to your advantage. It's not just going to be given to you. Even in college you're still competing with folks just out of high school that are really sharp. It's not going to be easy, but through hard work and dedication you will get there. Some of the same principles that you used to be successful in the military will transition you well into civilian life.

Jim, I thank you for your service and for contributing to this effort.

Chapter 5: Be Aware

*Meet **Jessica Scott**, a Kansan, and an Active Duty Air Force Veteran*

Jessica, again thank you for just for your service and for being available for this project. Share your background about where you grew up, your hometown experience and the path that led you into the military.

I grew up in a small town called Emporia in middle of Kansas. Nothing really there as far as the economy goes. After high school I initially decided to join the military. I wanted to be an air traffic controller. But I got stupid. I was in love, got married then got divorced three months later. I attempted to go to college and figured out it was way too expensive.

I didn't know how I was going to pay for it and decided to move to Wichita, Kansas where my dad lived

I had a job making twelve dollars an hour. It wasn't enough to really live on and I didn't have the time to go to college. One night I was lying in bed after I came off shift and heard how the military allowed laser eye surgery. My eyesight had been too bad to do air traffic control. So I decided to enlist in the military into whatever field would be open to me, get my eyes fixed, and then move into air traffic control. I was only going stay in as long as I needed to pay back that particular surgery and then I was going to be done. Ten years later here I am still in. My eyes are fixed, I am still in my original career field and I'm loving it.

I am a mental health technician and I specialize in substance abuse. I have obtained my national alcohol drug abuse certification. So if I wanted to leave the Air Force, I could go work on an in-patient unit and carry my own caseloads.

I applaud you for being in a field

that I know has a lot of need and takes some special people. When you first came into the military, was there anything that caught you off guard, surprises or things that maybe you weren't prepared?

You know I feel really lucky because my recruiter was exceptional. Every question I asked, he was a hundred percent upfront with me. I had no issues with him. To this day I've got him on my Facebook page. I still talk to him. He retired as a senior master sergeant. He's an incredible support for me. His being so upfront prepared me for what I was getting into. People around me and the people who were training me were incredible.

Let's talk about your deployment experience.

I served in the Contingency Aeromedical Staging Facility (CSAF) located in Balad Iraq. The CASF aerovaced out wounded warriors. My job was to make sure that they were all comfortable for their transports and offered them an outlet to talk if they needed it. I was also in charge of taking care of the 14% who came in specifically to be aerovaced out due to mental health concerns. I was tasked with making 100% contact with every wounded soldier, not just those specifically assigned to mental health. Because of the current Aerovac system, we are able to get soldiers to healthcare within 24 hours of being injured which is drastically reducing the fatality rate. It was a very intense experience...heartbreaking...but also very rewarding.

Do you yourself suffer from any wounds or injuries that classify you as a Wounded Warrior?

I experience PTSD-like symptoms. Loud noises will at times unnerve me. Its sporadic things that pop up. But as long as I can keep myself away from them, I'm okay.

What would you say was your darkest moment or the deepest challenge that you have had?

You know I don't think I can pick out a specific instance. My little brother was over there at the same time. He was an Army infantry soldier who came back and suffered from severe PTSD. While he was deployed, I was constantly looking in the faces of the men and women I was transporting out of the AOR to make sure it wasn't my brother. I wanted to be able to tell my Mom first, before she heard it from someone else. That was a difficult time.

You're in a field of work where you see individuals struggling, maybe through poor decisions on their own part, maybe through others things that have happened to them. I speak with business owners who have formed their opinion about veterans from what they see in the media. What would you want business owners to keep in mind when it comes to hiring veterans?

The one thing that drives me absolutely crazy is that the media typically portrays the extreme cases of behavior when it comes to veterans. Most veterans are not like that.

If you were giving soldiers and service members advice and trying to get their attention on what they need to be paying attention to in terms of balancing their life, for making good choices, what would you want them to be paying attention to?

They need to be aware of the signs or symptoms of PTSD or other similar issues. If they see any of those symptoms, they should take the risk of visiting a mental health professional. Yes...it's usually very scary to go sit down with somebody you don't know and speak about all the things that are bothering you. But hopefully they will find some sort of peace with whatever is going on by getting some help.

I know in the Air Force when it comes to this sort of stuff, typically about ninety seven percent of the people who visit mental health experience no job repercussions. It's when they try to gut it out and not pay attention, by trying be the tough guys. That is when things get worse, like a snowball rolling downhill. Then their commanders take notice. Then they get command-directed in and then their commanders have access to all of that information. By going on their own volition, they can get the needed care and avoid command involvement.

You shared that you have over ten years in the service. So what do you look to accomplish and achieve over the next five ten years?

Right now I'm a freshman in college and I love it. I'm working full time. I'm taking as many credit hours as I can to attempt to get my bachelors. I have already gotten my associates degree. My career field is mental health services. I'm a student at the University of Colorado, Colorado Springs.

I want to put this information to work in my career. It's my goal after the military to go into teaching. My favorite teacher ever was my speech teacher in high school and I was the novice forensic team and that's what I want to do. I want get involved in high school speech and novice forensics and do something completely different and have a job where I get to have fun rather than be so serious all the time.

I will say you will have earned that indeed. Thank you for what you are doing for our service members and for our country. Your story is one of resilience.

Thank you for giving me the opportunity to tell it.

Chapter 6: Keep Your Mind on the Greater Good

*Meet **Bonnie Silver**, a Chicagoan, Army Veteran, now serving as a not-for-profit consultant*

Let's just talk about your background - talk about your hometown.

I am originally from a suburb of Chicago. My family relocated to Florida when I graduated high school. After a short time in Florida, I soon became a flight attendant with Eastern Airlines. About a year into working with Eastern, they went bankrupt and went out of business. I stayed in Florida for a bit and then relocated to Arlington, Texas but in less than a year, I found myself heading back to my hometown outside of Chicago and I was kind of lost.

Upon getting settled back home, I took a few college classes as I just didn't know what I wanted to do with my life. One day, I was talking to my brother, Scott, on the phone of which at the time he was an active duty Marine who had recently returned from combat in Desert Storm. I was sharing with him that I felt that I was lacking discipline and direction. As my older brother he was giving me advice and his advice was to look into the military. I never thought of joining the military until this point in my life. So, at twenty three, I took his advice and started looking at the various branches of service, as an option.

The following week, I went down to the recruiting office and originally met with the Marine Corps recruiter. I ended up taking my ASVAB with the Marine Corps. I then met with the Air Force recruiter, as well as the Navy recruiter but it wasn't until I met with Adam Williams, the Army recruiter, that I actually felt that I could join the military. He made it easy, stating that I could pick my job and only needed to initially do a two-year active duty commitment. This plan appealed to me so I picked Supply as my MOS and signed up for an initial two-year enlistment. I trusted him completely and fortunately he followed through on everything that he told me and we are still friends till this day.

So, I joined the Army under the delayed entry program in the fall of 1991 and then entered the service and headed to basic training on January 14, 1992. Honestly it was one of the best decisions of my life. Much of my confidence and self-esteem have come from my military experience. So I am a huge proponent and advocate for the military as I know the benefits of it. To this day, I am actively involved with our military and veterans. I don't care what branch, what rank or what era, we are all connected. We all served!

Okay, so you're initial training took place where?

I did my basic training at Fort Jackson, South Carolina. I joined as a supply specialist. My first assignment was working as part of the cadre in an AIT unit.

After the initial months of service, were there any surprises? Was there anything caught you off guard about the military experience? Did you experience anything that you were not quite prepared for?

The hardest part for me, quite honestly, was living in the barracks with other women. Being twenty-three, I had lived on my own and was older than most of the other trainees that were right out of high school and came straight from living with their parents. I could handle the drill sergeants and discipline. I even could handle all of the physical demands, responsibilities and expectations but dealing with many of these other females drove me crazy as there was a lot of immaturity and pettiness that I couldn't relate to. I befriended another gal that was around my age and we became fast friends.

There was one area that intimidated me and actually incited fear and that was qualifying with my weapon. Ironically, I ended up qualifying as an expert and weapons qualifications ended up being one of my favorite experiences in the military.

So, looking back, it was overcoming fear (False Evidence Appearing Real). For me personally, I feel that I had an advantage during basic training as being a little older and having worked in the civilian sector and living on my own gave me more preparation for the major adaptations and changes that come with joining the military.

How many years were you in the service?

I served a total of six and a half years with my training. After my initial two year enlistment, I re-enlisted for another two years and then again for another two years.

I had a great military experience

and quite honestly I love what the military did for me and all that the military represents: duty, honor, selfless service. I love the sense of camaraderie, the structure and the respect. I also loved the majority of my fellow soldiers that I worked with and find that the majority of my closest friends were those that I served with here and abroad.

There were so many positives of my military experience. I loved it so much that I actually wanted to become a recruiter. In fact, I had submitted my packet to become a recruiter upon coming back stateside from my deployment. This was now 1997/1998 time-frame and they were in dire need of recruiters, especially female recruiters as not many people volunteered for this duty. My goal was to transfer my supply MOS to the recruiter MOS.

My recruiter packet was impeccably prepared and I had everything in line for what they needed to approve my packet. I was completely confident that I would get picked up as a recruiter. The only thing that I was dealing with while on deployment was wrist pain and had a pending surgery scheduled upon going back stateside. Well, much to my surprise, I got my recruiter packet back toward the end of my deployment and was shocked to read that it was denied. The reason was they didn't want a medical issue on their hands. Honestly, I couldn't believe they rejected the packet due to wrist surgery. I had been so excited about this new path but now everything changed. I had to regroup and recover. That plan was no longer an option but I was determined to move forward and as much as I loved the military, I felt this was a sign that it was time to exit the service. I truly believe that I would have been an amazing recruiter but it obviously wasn't meant to be.

I had pinned all of my hopes in this opportunity as I really didn't have the option to go back to Ft. Bliss and resume my life there. Another reason why high hopes on becoming a recruiter was that it would give me an opportunity to move and have a fresh start somewhere new. What I haven't mentioned yet, was that I had been married at the time of my deployment. While on deployment, he had established a relationship with my then best friend and moved her into our home. So, upon returning from deployment, I came back to divorce papers and having to start all over. But everything happens for a reason and since becoming a recruiter didn't pan out, I opted to move forward with the medical board and becoming medically honorably discharged for my wrist, asthma and thyroid disease. Interestingly, I was discharged from the service on July 27, 1998 which was actually my ETS (Expiration Term of Service) date.

Looking back at those experiences, what would you say was your deepest challenge? What was a dark moment or the darkest moment for you?

For me it was being rejected as a recruiter as that was a tough pill to swallow. I obviously wanted to do it for numerous reasons and truly felt it was my calling, so it was disappointing, to say the least, to be rejected.

I also had other challenges. Mostly contending with being sexually harassed. It started pretty early on with a Drill Sergeant while in AIT and then there were other incidents throughout my military career from fellow soldiers to senior enlisted personnel. Fortunately, I was capable of handling the situations and none ever escalated to anything beyond harassment

When you left the service, talk about your transition. Talk about how you transitioned to the work that you are now doing.

I had a really challenging transition as I was dealing with the end of my marriage, leaving the military and relocation from Texas to Florida, all at one time.

I am pretty resilient and I went with it. A big issue that I had to deal with was the lack of respect I noticed in civilian life. I really I struggled with that. I obtained a job with a professional services company. They ended up selling the business. During this time period I was utilizing my GI Bill educational benefits of which I am a huge proponent for and I coach a lot of transitioning members on this. If you have the free education, take advantage of it. So I went ahead and I got my bachelor's degree and then went on to earn my MBA. When this company sold out, I ended up getting my Real Estate license and unfortunately, due to the lack of loyalty in the industry, I only lasted eight months. It was not a great experience for me but it did lead me to my next opportunity. Having worked Real Estate, I had noticed a lack of storage and closet space so I wanted to help fill that need of maximizing space so I ended up starting my own business and became a distributor for a garage organizing, space saving system and I loved it. I found that I could work for myself and serve my customers with the kind of loyalty, diligence and service that I was accustomed to from the military. During this time-frame I had remarried, got pregnant and moved back to Chicago where I am from originally. After a little over four years, my priorities changed and I now wanted to focus on parenting also noting not too many people organize their garages in Chicago, so I closed my business. Then after only two years back in Chicago, we moved again but to the West Coast where we currently reside. We have since divorced but we are on great terms and get along well as we share custody of our son who is now ten years old.

When my son was four, I decided to return to the workforce and went into sales. I worked remotely and toward the end of 2008, I was downsized when they let all the outside sales personnel go and now found myself unemployed. As a single parent, living in Southern California, I struggled financially. I spent the three years while I was unemployed doing a lot of volunteer work and writing. It was a struggle having my MBA and being a veteran and not being able to secure a decent paying job that I could live on. Fortunately, my time of service set me up for the job I have now working with a non-profit, as well as taking the time to write, I was able to become a contributor to a Best Selling book. One of my favorite sayings is that "God hides his blessings in adversity to surprise us with his love" and that was the case for me during the three years of unemployment.

I had been consulting and working with Project HIRED, a 501(c)3, not-for-profit organization, which maintains a single vision: to be a significant force for the employment of individuals with disabilities until the need no longer exists. Since 1978, we have been serving adults with disabilities, including disabled warriors, and have placed thousands into jobs in the local and surrounding communities and nationally.

The Project HIRED Wounded Warrior Workforce Program also supports employers of veterans with disabilities by providing HR support, management training, and consulting services or a non-profit that serves the Wounded Warrior community. I'm very passionate about trying to help people to not go through what I went through being unemployed. So working in this capacity had allowed me to serve to assist others. When the funding didn't come through to extend my contract, other doors opened to support a few other non-profits, such as Hire a Patriot (www.hireapatriot.org), as well as Military Musters (www.militarymusters.org). Both organizations allow me to use my skill set and expertise to best serve our military and veterans.

So you're personally involved with working with the veteran community as well as other communities.

Yes, as a consultant for several non-profits, I do outreach at the locally at the VA Hospitals, Camp Pendleton, Balboa, job fairs etc. Since I am out in the community, I have built up my network so that I can best assist anyone that I come in contact with so whatever their needs are, I can refer them to the resources that can best assist them nationally. My mission is to help everyone to the best of my abilities as I don't want anyone to feel alone and there are enough resources out there to help everyone in pretty much every situation.

If you were talking to business owners today about veterans, disabled veterans and wounded warriors, what message what you want to tell business owners about that community?

I generally start by asking questions such as: "Would you consider hiring a Veteran?" Fortunately, most respond with a resounding, "yes." However for those that reply with concerns, I inquire what those concerns may be and reply accordingly.

Sometimes hiring managers are concerned with the Veterans lack of education. I challenge them with the life skills brought from a recent college graduate that has the piece of paper versus the Veteran with 4 plus years of on-the-job training, managerial experience, teamwork, mission and goal-oriented background, as well as overall knowledge in a variety of capacities that might be the equivalent of a senior level manager in some instances. Our military has invested the money and time to instill the core values of leadership into every military member. The civilian sector doesn't invest in its staff to become leaders, per se, so companies can train anyone to do a job but leadership is automatically a given when hiring a Veteran. In my experience, a veteran is someone who would be way more qualified for the majority of jobs and positions while being an asset to the team. An added benefit at this juncture is the amazing tax benefits that a company receives for hiring this Veteran, someone who has given so much to protect you and our country. In my opinion, the tax incentive is just an added bonus and pales into comparison to everything else that is gained by hiring a Veteran.

As you look out over the next few years, what do you hope to achieve?

I am working on a few book projects to share my experiences and provide positive inspiration to others. I love to write, it is truly a passion of mine. I will also continue to serve as that is paramount to me. So right now, I consult with and also volunteer with several military and Veteran organizations, as well as some other community foundations. My personal mission statement is to make a positive footprint here on this earth by doing good deeds, helping others and consistently 'paying it forward.'

Is there any final thought, anything that you'd want the business community or the veteran community to know?

My request is for Veterans to ask for assistance and then actually receive it. There are plenty of people that care and organizations that have a variety of services but it takes the Veteran to make the first move. You have served your country now let your country serve you. Let other's actually help you if you need it and lastly, offer your help to someone less fortunate. By giving to others', it helps one to keep perspective and stay out of their pity party.

For the business community, the best decision you could make is to hire a veteran because you going to get the quality, the caliber, the leadership, and the camaraderie. It's going to be one of the best decisions you've ever made. Veterans aren't looking for a handout, just a hand up to be the best they can be. Give them a chance and see the results!

Well my let me just say thank you again for your service what you've done what you're doing.

I want to add one other thing for the veterans. Go visit or support or show your support in any manner to a fellow veteran. Become a part of the team. If you feel isolated, go and be around like minds. Keep your mind on the greater good. Thank you, Kevin, for this opportunity.

Chapter 7: It's The Mentality

*Meet **Josh Winget**, Texan, combat Army Veteran, now serving in the business community*

Tell us about your background, your hometown, and your reason for joining the military?

I graduated high school down here in Cahill, Texas. I enlisted in March 2006. I actually moved from Cahill to Denver to spend the last six months before I enlisted with my father. I always wanted to be a soldier. I always wanted to serve my country and help out and change the world in any way I can for the better.

When 9/11 hit, what grade were you in at the time and how did that impact you as you think back to that event?

Josh: I was a junior in high school at the time. It really was a shock. I couldn't believe that it happened. That was the only thing that was on the news over and over again. It really hit me hard.

Looking back at your entrance into the Army and afterwards, did anything catch you by surprise? Was there anything that you were not prepared for?

I knew I wanted to be with the Infantry, on the frontline. I knew that it was going to be intense. It was pretty much everything I expected.

How long were you in the Army?

I was in the Army just about 4 years.

So walk us through to the point when you were deployed.

I deployed in 2006 and that was right before the surge. I was only there for roughly two months. It was very fast, very intense training. It doesn't stop at basic. You have to learn your unit protocols and your rules of engagement. I had to get to know them very fast. In terms of our deployment, we were there roughly about fifteen months.

Are you also a wounded warrior? Did you suffer any wounds over in Iraq?

Yes ... I was a 240 gunner in my team. I was on the track with 240, the main machine gun, but my track directly came under 11 IED attacks. Those attacks resulted in my experiencing brain damage. I was awarded the Purple Heart. I began to suffer from headaches, nausea and other types of TBI symptoms for the last seven months of our deployment.

Is there anything you would want people to know about the

experience you had in being attacked by IEDs and the resulting effects?

It's hard to understand. It's hard to describe your real emotions and everything that's going through your head when the bomb goes off and destroys the front end of your track. It's really hard to explain all the different emotions. I mean you don't even know if you are hurt, if you still receiving fire, who's alive, who's dead, and who's hurt.

What has been your darkest moment or your deepest challenge since those experiences up until today?

Some of the deepest challenges, of course, were losing close brothers in arms. But probably the hardest thing I ever had to experience was watching my unit redeploy to Afghanistan without me. I was not able to redeploy because of my being diagnosed with TBI (traumatic brain injury). That was one of the hardest things I ever had to do in my entire life, knowing that they're going into the heat of it without me. That day was the hardest thing I ever had to experience.

You hold your head high for what you did for the United States. I want you to know that. Let me kind of switch perspectives a little bit here and let's look ahead. You transitioned out of the military after you returned. When did you leave the military?

September 2009. I had transitioned from to the Wounded Warriors Unit. That's where I went through my medical work process.

What have been some of the big challenges or big hurdles that you experienced in making that transition?

The initial transition was extremely difficult because I was leaving not just my unit but I was leaving the Army. The Army was my life. I was planning to be a 20 year man. Now, having left the Army, I didn't have that unit camaraderie and understanding of my fellow soldiers on a daily basis. I was back home with my family and friends. But I couldn't talk to them. If I did talk to them, they had no idea what I was talking about.

Talk to me about how that transition has gone for you. I'd like to hear about what is going well and what has not gone well.

I've been trying to get into a new career or into different businesses here in the civilian sector. It's extremely difficult for soldiers. It's as if we speak different languages. Translating what we did in combat or in the military is extremely difficult. So it's hard to know who you can trust to understand you when presenting your military background.

Tell us about your family.

I'm happily married to a very beautiful bride Jessica. We have a son named Trevor.

Share with us how it has been for you and your family over the last

few years since your transition into civilian life.

Well over the last couple of years I have dedicated my time to my schooling. I have been using my GI Bill to complete my bachelors degree in management. I had to go back to school because my infantry background did not translate to anything in the civilian sector. So I came to realize that I needed to further my education. I'm actually considering extending my education to an MBA.

If I brought you into a room and you had a number business owners who have expressed some degree of interest in working with soldiers, what would you want them to know and understand about soldiers like yourself when it comes to working with you and opening up opportunities for you?

I would stress that we have such a disciplined nature instilled in our minds. We are quick to listen. We are quick to learn. You give us something to do and we won't stop until it's done. It's the mentality that all military personnel have. I think that's missing from some the mindset of some employers. We have leadership skills that cannot be understated.

We think outside the box. We just don't see one way of getting something done when given a task.

What do want to accomplish as you move through this new season here in your life?

I want to find a career that gives me some form of purpose again. When I was in the military, I always felt like I was doing something that I was needed for. I want that back. I want to feel like am doing something accomplished. I want to contribute.

Regarding the resources that are available for transitioning to civilian life, what would you want today's veterans to know and be aware of?

I have had tremendous experience with the Wounded Warrior Project. They have been unbelievably helpful to me with my transition, getting me reconnected with different veterans, getting that camaraderie back.

I don't want to speak ill of anybody but I know that there is an issue with different organizations working with each other because they seem threatened by each other for federal funding, especially for the VA. They should work together instead of trying to compete against each other.

Is there anything else about veterans that you think the business community should take the time to understand? You talked about how discipline and other attributes of being a soldier can strengthen an organization. Is there anything else that you feel may be a gap between the veteran community and the business community?

Well one thing that comes to mind is the gap of understanding about the certain conditions or disabilities that veterans are coming back from the war with. One that really pops up in my head is of course the post-traumatic stress disorder. I think that there is a huge stigma especially that came from the media. What the public in general needs to realize is that post-traumatic stress disorder doesn't mean that these individuals are crazy or they are mentally unstable.

There is a large misunderstanding about the different disabilities that people are coming home with. Many believe that these disabled vets cannot function well. I graduated from my university with a four year degree that I finished in three years. I graduated with a 3.7 GPA and continued with my MBA. And I suffered from traumatic brain injury. Veterans can be diagnosed with something and still be very capable.

Given that you completed your four year degree in three years with almost a 4.0 GPA, are you finding still that the diagnosis that you came out of the military with is hindering you in some way?

Unfortunately it does. In trying to access the job market, every time I go to apply or submit my resume to a large corporation, they ask about my veteran status. From there the fact that I am diagnosed with a disability usually comes up. Usually from that point, the discussion does not go very far.

Is your gut telling you that you are being shut off from any more opportunity to communicate with those companies?

Yes...it's really my gut and I really get that feeling from some of the people that I have met face to face.

Where do you see yourself in the next five or so years?

Where I want to be five years down the road is in a career where I can work hard and do something productive, hopefully find something in a career whereby I can contribute back to society, find a sense of purpose as I had in the military. I want to be in a place where I don't have to worry about my family's well-being and am taking care of them.

As I wrap this I want to say thank you for putting yourself in harm's way, for stepping into the arena for this country. I don't detect an ounce of bitterness from you. You have struggled through what you needed to struggle through and now you are moving on to this next new season. I can't thank you enough for what you have done. I want to encourage you as you move through this. It is just a matter of continuing to take your God given abilities and applying them.

I will...thank you for giving me the opportunity to tell my story.

Chapter 8: Loyalty Isn't a Punch Line

*Meet **James Zazueta**, Californian, Air Force Veteran, now serving in the security industry*

James, share your background, your hometown background, family time experience and kind of take us down the road of what led you into the military.

I'm from a kind of a smaller town, Indio, California, about 20 miles away from Palm Springs. My mom had me at a younger age. I think she was 19. My dad was about 18. I went to school locally. Parents split up when I was nine and after that I stayed with mom and we moved around quite a bit. My mom was always supportive and she always pushed us to do good, but she never had...how do I say, expectations that were astronomical or anything like that. She always said "Do good in life. Whatever you guys want to do, just do good in life and be good people." People always asked me "Why did you want to join the military?" and I can honestly say, from the time I was a little boy, it was the only thing I ever wanted to do. I remember when I was a kid, watching Top Gun on VHS over and over again, me and my little brother. Me and my little brother would pop it into the VCR and turn on the stereo and just blast it. And ever since then, I always had a fascination with airplanes. That was my thing. I always loved airplanes. I always watched the old WW II documentaries on dog fights and kept up with all the latest fighters.

So when the time came in high school to start thinking about life after high school and what you were going to do for a career, I took a test that indicated I was qualified to go into the Air Force. I said "Hey, this is something that might be pretty cool! Air Force has got airplanes." So, I met with a recruiter who went through the entire process. Since I was 17, I had to get my mom's permission to do it and that was not easy.

After I entered and received my training, I was stationed in Fairfield, CA. I didn't get deployed until 2005. The end of 2004-beginning of 2005 was when the really big insurgency in Iraq happened. The whole Fallujah offensive happened. The ops tempo was crazy. I mean, we couldn't keep jets on the ground long enough to fix them, so a lot of rules were being bent, which was my case when I deployed in May 2005. Everybody was spread thin, so I did my first trip in the summer of 2005. I was at Balad air base, Iraq. The Army called it LSA Anaconda, I believe. It was just outside the town of Balad right off the Tiger's River. I believe it was about 30-40 miles north of Baghdad, so it's pretty much in the heart of the Sunni triangle. Curtis Fluitt and I were both in Iraq together. It just so happened it was both our first deployment.

I deployed twice and left the service in 2007.

What was your most challenging or darkest moment during your time in the service?

I would say the darkest times I had while I was in the Air Force were probably during my deployments to Iraq. Not so much the first one. But the second one was a little bit worse because at the time I was in a relationship with a girl and she ended up seeing somebody else during the time I was deployed. It seemed like everybody went through some kind of relationship problem. I think that was the biggest issue for everyone while we were there. And this is when we were gone for only four months. I could just imagine how bad it was for our soldiers and our marines that were gone for 12-18 months. The public doesn't understand the strain that it can put on a family, which was one of my reasons why I decided to leave the military.

As you look back at that, what would you tell service members today

who are about to step into that situation wherein they will be separated from their family or loved ones? What would you say to them?

Communicate, absolutely 100% communicate. Communication. One of my biggest problems at the time was I would not verbally express what I might have been feeling inside. It may be a machismo thing that I think a lot of men in particular might have. But I remember at the time, when I was leaving the woman that I was seeing, she would always ask "What's the matter? What's the matter? What's the matter?" and my answer was always "Nothing, nothing, nothing's going on." When really you have a million and one things in your head, but you don't talk about it. As a service member I would say sit down, talk to your family, let them know what's going on. Let them know how your feel. Have their family tell them what scares them, what makes them anxious so you can talk about it and maybe the talking will help get you through it before you leave.

Now on the part of command...make every outlet available to your service men and women to stay in contact with their families at home. And today it's...I think it's so much better today with all of the technology outlets. Now I talk to my friend and he's got telephone, he's got e-mails, Facebook. I think he said he even has Wi-Fi in his room, which is wonderful. He can sit in his room while he's deployed and Skype with his family.

Let me tell you something that I heard and let me get your reaction to this as candidly as you want to be. One of the things I've heard is yes, skyping, Facebook, G-chatting, all the different ways that people can communicate have been wonderful ways for families to communicate with a deployed family member. The other side of this real-time communication coin is that it can be a negative if the service member and/or family member or loved one do not know how to communicate about the issues that they're facing and dealing with. I've heard about families

where the spouse is deployed, communicating with his/her spouse and the discussion gets into issues that the deployed member can really do nothing about...kids bad behavior, extended family issues, etc. Just things that life would normally bring anyway. It makes it difficult because now the family member who's deployed is dealing with the frustration of the spouse who's back home and there's not much they can do. So I'd be interested to get your thoughts on this.

I absolutely agree that that can happen and I see how that can happen. Going back to my friend that just recently deployed, I'm great friends with his family. We both were at Travis together, we started the Air Force together, so I'm great friends with his wife also and I don't worry so much about him because I know he knows what to do. He's a professional; he knows how to handle it. He's done it before. His wife on the other hand...I mean, this is his second deployment in nine years, so they're not used to this and now they have small kids and this was actually...it's funny that you mentioned that, because it's actually something I brought up with her one day when I was speaking to her. I said "You know what, I understand that..." and she's just that kind of person...she would not bring those issues to him during conversation because she would rather keep it inside and let it build up within her and let it be her problem than have him worry about it, when there is absolutely nothing he can do about it. And for the most part I agree with that. A distracted soldier is a dead soldier. I 100% agree with that. When they're gone, they need to concentrate on doing what they've got to do and getting back home. On the other hand, for those that are at home, they need outlets at home that they can talk to.

Talk about how your own transition from the service into civilian life.

You know, it's rough. I'm not going to lie. Everybody always tells you it's going to be rough transitioning, getting used to being a civilian. While I was in, being the person that I was then and the way I think a lot of young men and women appear, but especially young men and women that are in the service, you shrug it off. "Don't know what you're talking about. I can deal with this. It's not that big of a deal! It's nothing. There's nothing wrong with me. I can go out and do it." It's not that easy. And you know, when I left, my behavior I can say was more erratic and immature than when I was younger. We've been at war going on 11 years now and that takes a toll. The last two years I was in the military I was gone for 356 days, so I was just gone. All the time just gone. And I returned from my last deployment in 2007 and as soon as I got back, I had to start out-processing. Looking back, I realize that it is important to never question your sense of purpose. You always have a purpose. There's always a mission. There's always something to do. Looking back, I didn't feel like I had a sense of purpose. After being part of something that's so much greater than you.

Everybody likes being praised and
awarded and rewarded. It makes you feel
good. I'm not going to lie. It makes
everybody feel good and to not have that
anymore, to go from that to not having
that...man, it's rough. And I went from
the military and I went straight into the
sheriff's department. I took a test, went
into the academy eight months after I left
the military and even law enforcement
being a paramilitary job, even that didn't
give me the sense of gratification that I
got from being in the military. You fight
feeling mediocre.

You went into law enforcement?

Yes, I was with the sheriff's
department for 13 months and the entire
time I was in, it was having this internal
battle. I'm serving the community. I'm
doing a good thing. It's a great job. It paid
great. I was getting paid more money
than I was paid in the military, great
benefits. But the entire time I was in, I
always felt like something was missing,
like something wasn't there. Maybe it
was because I had been so busy before
with the op tempo of being in the
military. I haven't had time to

decompress. Whatever it may have been, it hindered my ability to be the best law enforcement officer that I could've been and I did eventually resign. I knew the entire time I was with the sheriff's department, I thought, "I'm better than this. I can be better than this." I knew my attitude was wrong, but I didn't know why because I never had that kind of attitude. I couldn't figure it out. I guess in my mind I just rationalized: "It's got to be the job. It must be the job." And that wasn't the case at all. I left that job and the last three years have been a great learning experience for me.

One of the things I learned is to not take things for granted. I think that's what it was. I took that whole law enforcement career for granted. The biggest issue was feeling like you didn't have a sense of purpose, like you weren't a part of something that was bigger than you, absolutely the camaraderie, the brotherhood. In the law enforcement community people like to talk about being in brotherhood. I thought, "Yeah, kind of, but you guys have no idea."

People that are in law enforcement that were in the military, that's a brotherhood. My friends I knew when I was at Travis, when I called them "brother", I meant it. They're my brothers. And you don't have that outside of the military. It's a big issue.

What are you currently doing?

I'm currently working private security at a country club and I've been doing that for the last three year. During the time I've been here I've actually been trying to get back into law enforcement and it's harder. This time it's tough.

You're in California again now?

Yes, sir. Back home in my hometown. Have come full circle.

If you were talking to some business people about service members, what would you want them to know? What are some of the things that you would enumerate to them that you would want business people to be aware of?

As an employee, a prior service member can be one of the most loyal people that you can probably have work for you, as long as the employer is of the fair type. It was my experience that when you had a supervisor that you felt was genuine, you went out of your way to be better, to go that extra mile so that your unit or your superior, your supervisor would look good. And I took pride in that. If my supervisor gets praised for something that is directly because of what I did or my unit did or my group or even the work now that we all do, it's a great sense. Veterans can be the most loyal people business owners ever met. Because I think a lot of people think loyalty is a punch line for the military people, but it really isn't. Loyalty is something that is taken very seriously. It's the nature of the business. When you're having to put your life on the line for your friends, your buddies and more, for your country, loyalty isn't a punch line. It's a backbone, it's a way of life, it's what you do. And I think a lot of employers in the civilian sector or in the business don't know that. I think that is probably what I would try to express the most.

Where do you want to go from here, James, the next phase three to five years? What would you like to be doing?

Now the biggest thing for me is just being the best husband, the best father I can be. I don't get it right all the time. When I don't, I make sure I work hard to get it right. That is the ultimate calling, service before self in the world and I'm absolutely grateful and blessed to be able to experience that through my family. But career wise, I made a mistake when I left law enforcement. I'm trying to get back into it. My wife's in law enforcement currently and I want to get back because it is a sense of service. It's one of those jobs too where, especially for prior service members, you never lose that sense of service, whether it be the country, the community, whatever it might be. You're going to always want to help people and help those that can't help themselves.

James, your story has contributed to my better understanding of the challenges that the vast majority of veterans face today. When I first started this book project, my focus was strictly wounded warriors and their stories. As I began to talk with the different soldiers and service members and just started down this path, the good Lord just opened up my mind, showing me that there were other things that are being told that people should hear.

Yes... I just didn't want to be part of another war story again. There' a million books out there that you can read about war stories. We've all got them. I have war stories but I didn't want it to be that. I want it to be about things the people don't know about because most of us are afraid of speaking about it because of the fear of people thinking you might be a weak person. I want to bring out things that people don't know or hear about. Everybody wants to know the bang-bang shoot-em-up story and the bombs and the blood. When really that stuff isn't what bothers you the most. I think when you're in that situation, you just deal with the fact. You get over it. It's the mental aspect of it that people don't understand and I would say going through the process of returning back home, the military has a lot of work to do with mental disorders for soldiers that are returning home. The military hasn't dealt with a situation like this since Vietnam.

You're right. You're absolutely right. I'm a Vietnam-era veteran. I did not go to Vietnam. I was in the service. I entered the service when I was just towards the end of Vietnam. I was in Korea as the U.S. was leaving Vietnam. I had the honor of having NCOs and soldiers who had gone and served multiple tours in Vietnam. So I got close to it in that regard. But looking back now, you're absolutely right. A generation later we really missed the boat. Thankfully, because we are doing what we're doing now, some of the benefit is also helping our Vietnam-era veterans.

Yes, it is great that they are getting help as well.

James, thanks again for what you did for the country. And for contributing so candidly to this project.

It was my privilege to do so. I hope it helps.

Epilogue

Thank you for investing your resources in this book. Hopefully these stories made a personal connection and have better informed you about what this latest generation of veterans have experienced. More importantly it is our hope that the public, and particularly the business community, will see this new generation in a different light...and better comprehend the value that they can bring to any organization.

If you are a veteran, avail yourself of any and all resources available, ask for help, and use the resilience that you have developed through your military experience to push ahead in the pursuit of your goals.

Other Books

*From Ops Center to Industry: Lessons
from the Arena of Leadership*

This book captures over 300 years
of cumulative leadership experience
through in-depth, personal interviews
with 11 retired military flag officers who
now serve as business executives. They
speak candidly about the challenges that
leaders face in today's fast-paced
business environment. They offer their
own views on how to raise up the next
generation of leaders, how to lead in the
current viral age of social media, and
provide their own personal reflections on
what they would have changed, knowing
what they know today. They include a
former Chief Information Officer for the
U.S. Army, a former commander of
"Patton's 3rd Army", and an inductee
into the West Point Army Sports Hall of
Fame.

Reflections from the C-Suite:
Opinions and Advice

This book provides a conversational and candid discussion with 8 business leaders who have served or are currently serving at the C-Level of corporate America. It has reached #1 bestseller status within Amazon's Organizational Change category and # 7 in its Leadership category.

Both books are available on Amazon.com

www.ingramcontent.com/pod-product-compliance
Lightning Source LLC
Chambersburg PA
CBHW061743020426
42331CB00006B/1345